THE UNION OF SHADOWS

chindah musashi

THE UNION OF SHADOWS

chindah musashi

astrum books

THE UNION OF SHADOWS

The Union of Shadows.

Dedicated to my family, without them I would not be inspired.

I

**Religion is a spawn of the ego
An excuse to dream awake
A means to silence the true God
Who resides inside of you.
God is man in Awareness**

II

We become what we are in the full moon
Dirty sexual Rabbits
That barks as dogs.
Vices forever forbidden like Eden's fruit.

III

She's an extraordinary woman
But a dreadful lover
A little mysterious and truly sweet.
Without you I'll be lost in a land of silence."Love itself is a harmless mental illness
But the unparalled intrusion of intimacy leaves love undone"

IV

Love is a powerful army
Secret, invisible and mighty
She blossoms at night
And wilts in the daylight.

V

I don't care much for material things
I just want to make love and write words.
Is sadness and beauty all there is to poetry?

VI

The trees spoke to me,
For me and through me
And the fairy flowered butterflies
Granted me gifts beyond this Domain.

VII

Gazelles know their place
It's the Lions that forget,
Like leaves all flesh can be eaten
And must be eaten.

"On who's account is justice to be considered"

IX

Democracy is a necessary illusion
For the ruler and the ruled
Any world ruled is an oppressed world.

X

We're either Venom or remedy
Man or woman
We're neither polar nor solar
Sun and moon.
We exist in phases and beyond phases

XI

What a deplorable place to be
Were leaving a legacy isn't paramount
A most dishonorable place indeed.

There's no word for damage
It's a lost language
Body dead, spirit left, Jesus wept.

XII

All the pretty faces turn ugly
Eclipsed by the gaze of truth
Nothing behind you is worthy
So, keep your vision true.

XIII

I will leave this place
And sojourn
I have made peace with my darkness
As I have with my light

I've buried my treasures deep
I'm not who I used to be
I traded him for a me more fulfilling

For a man worth rewarding

"I despise the beguile of the rat race
I'd rather go with the sun rays"

XIV
I prefer the weirdos and sinners
I prefer the religiously condemned
Their hearts lack laws so there's room for love
Spawns of the Moon, Earth and Stars.

XV
Happiness is something we never truly possessLike all truly beautiful things
She's infinite, a figment of our imagination.
What we truly desire is peace.
This is the path home
This path we walk alone.

XVI

The unique presence of us
Filled with triumph and loss
Sold our people for a cross
To hang our sins and forget our flaws

“Religion Pioneered slavery
There’s no God within it”

XVII

I struggled for breath on my old Aztec
Patterned bed sheet
feeling my heartbeat sporadically,
As universal essence left this plant

I felt ease, swimming in bliss
No happiness yet no melancholy.

A most peaceful experience
All the noise tranquil.

"Famines bring Banquets"

XVIII

Quick as shadows we must be
Night has been my dreams at dark.
A sleepless malice,
Turning, twisting and yearning
The crownless again shall be king.
Once you embrace death you gain life
To find us naked in the dark.

XIX

Let us create an Organization
That prioritizes the liberation
Of the spirit in this modern plane
She would stand in liberty of the
Incomprehensible.
There is a universal purpose to life,
That it is to be lived.

It is known that man has not seen the unprinted Snow –

But wished God's on Rocks and Symbols
To explain the divine ignorance
That plagues his genius mind.

XX

Language is inadequate to express these wonders.
Like the Gods I sing silent praises
How do I explain this vision?
From mind I see minds
From eyes I see light
I am dead and, in the womb,
I am the water experiencing the human feet
I am the sunlight where hippos bask.
I am the seed and the living fruit.

XXI

You're my Oasis in the desert

THE sweet Ocean breeze

THE Moonlight ever so pleasant

That beckons me to my knees.

"There's nothing more beautiful than the rising sun
Except a smile and the heart, you share it with"

XXII

Are you thinking about something sad?
It's a dreadful beautiful world.
And dark clothes look so sad, don't they?
I'm delighted to be sad
I pay homage and gain knowledge

XXIII

The past is a lake of stagnant water
Poisonous to he who drinks
Every second of life's search is an encounter with eternity.
A dance with God.

XXIV

What's the freedom of being nobody?
To wander in wonder
From tribe to tribe.
To be a person but a lot of beings
To see a multitude of sins unseen
To be foreign yet familiar.

XXV

Your dreams would become a spear
And a nightmare
Your yield and your shield.

XXVI

There's a dark place
Where evil sits in slumber
And Chaos relieved peace
I saw
The mighty neem trees
Crowned in Carbon.
Cut down for fire
In the darkest of Nights.

"Cities are human poultry farms"

XXVII

When I was alone
You were by my side,
You loved me.
I would love you in death
And beyond

XXVIII

These are letters of my soul
Diarized in ink
Stillness is the key to the empty place
There's an abundance of excess in this empty place
The wind knows the truth
The wind knows it all.

XXIX

Solitude and a field of corn
Is all I wish to see at dawn.
All the lovers I have shunned,
Broken hearts with pain profound
That keeps one bittersweet

"There's a language long forgotten
An unspoken language of the earth"

XXX

Long ago I heard a wonderful story
From a lady with a heart of Gold
Hands as gentle as the midnight breeze.
"When you do something for the ones you love
Instead of for the world, it's easier to decide
What must be done".

XXXI

Sex, lies and Oddities

The moment she walked through the door
I could see her beyond the surface of her crude
Rancor
Beneath her Mary gown and wooly hair
She had a rotten secret
She is a dirty little slut

“Beauty is the Great Seducer
With a tiger belly
and poisonous eyes”

XXXII

I don’t know why she
Comes to my sleep
As clear to me as the desert breeze
When I was hiding,you found me.
I see nothing without your permission

“The greatest grievance of all is watching
Your dreams become an illusion”.

XXXIII

Love is the sustained manifestation
Of the God we worship least
The creator of the naked beast
A tiger in a flooded street.

XXXIV

I want to live around tall and mighty trees
That breathes air to fill my lungs
Where sickness doesn't grow but rot
I'm not a witness I'm a living God

XXXV

"I am a host to a savage God in waiting
This oddity that I am despises fear
Ignores limitations and confronts hope"

The most of life is found In the Grey lines
The untraveled paths
The thunderous storms and rocky Gullies.
As we traverse to find peace within
We explore to help us endure

"I am the blackbird gliding without perch
A warm friend to the seas that tide humanity –

If modern reality is not soon abandoned
Fiction would rule society
We are not real but copies of ourselves"

XXXVI

"We're the wisdom of the universe
Made manifest in conscious form
When we abandon this form
We do not return, because we never left"

"I want to fall in love, but I'm bored
Of everyone I meet.

XXVII

What is Pretty?
The smell of life flowing out
The scent of Iron rust and sea water
The taste of a man's last gasp.

"At the seat of the soul, a monster so
Revered my demons call her peace".

XXXVIII

I wish I was at good at love
As I am at working
I wish I didn't leave people behind
I wish I could stay still and not be different
Words are nothing if not expressed
Expressions are regrets I wish I had.

XXXIX

If I die may I not die
In the arms of my love
For all it brightens love cast long shadows

XL

As the Sun and Moon endures
My love will adorn you
If it lacks depth, I'll go to the sea
If it lacks life, I'll speak to the leaves
You're the star and the wish come through

XLI

Let death itself teach you that you
Have no claim over love.
When the night set in with rain
Came the savage plundering devils
Who solemnly swore to honor themselves.
How astounding, not being bound by anyone
I go on ahead, to an even higher summit.

XLII

I've decided to have no reason,
I've decided to have no purpose at all
To just drift like dust particles smashing
Into butterflies that I find to be drifting as well

Maybe I'll follow the south breeze
I'll follow her as far as I can
To the top of the mountains,

I'll see caves and plant trees
I'll go as far as a man.

I'll watch the cows grazing
And eat with the wolves.
I'm dreaming myself a grand adventure
To have no dreams at all.

XLIII

There's a certain war that kills peace
In the morning when the cock crows
Footsteps leaving prints of thoughts
Daily dreams by reality crushed
Comfort Dead. A long-lost friend.

"No matter how many times you get up fighting
A bird crawling on the ground is nothing but food".

"I sat in the Garden on a half wet chair
With thoughts of the perfect love,

A love forever and more".

XLIV

Fill me with mourning
Till I have no use for love
I will offend you
And shatter your futures hope.
When your spirit is broken
And your sweet love is dead
I will quench your pain
And love you again.

XLV

I am the forceful flame
That unleashes the wind
In the days when the earth
Rose to the firmament ....
I am the chaos under heaven
That carves a maze through time
I am an ambitious mind

I love to be myself and I have so many
selves to be".

XLVI

You're pretending, aren't you?
Pretending to be kind
Pretending to be troubled
Pretending to love
I'm not any bitter
But I can't see you
I need to see you.
What's essential is visible to the heart

XLVII

I built a Garden for just us two
Within my heart, within my Soul.
Whenever I miss you, they flourish and bloom
You're always by me well pruned and regaled.

"I imagine I've loved you in a thousand
Lives before"

XLVIII

In solitude I opened my eyes to my heart.
That I listen to the harmonious pleasures
Of the breeze that sings sweet silence,
That my ear is deaf to her majestic songs.

That I am remembered as the tree and the
Leaves and the root,

That I am all things and nothing
Uniquely mundane

That I am what I am and what I would be
In eternal infinite, beyond self and legions,
Tribes and religions.
That cast doubt on Gods who speak this
Silent message: God is dead without man
And society is the killer of men.

XLIX

"Brick is earth compounded"
Life is soul expounded
The digger of Gold is the butcher of land

"I've often thought societal norms like religion
Is an intangible form of heroine".

L

Before all thoughts and Norms
Before morality and rationality
Humans are born with a liberty
To live within our own sun
And burn with a blinding brightness.

But righteousness is the corruption to our
Humanness
A rot so despicable it erodes your access
To doubt
God is man in Awareness

LI

When time has consumed all of me
Pleasure and pain
I would become an Ode the voices sing
A tale to mourn and drink
Would they say I did wrong?
Or the best he could?

Who would cherish me eternally?
Don't let such time pass, sing for me!
Sing sweet songs in the mighty now
When I am dead and amongst the stars
I would become a song,
I'll hear sweet songs of deeds
I'll know they sing for me.

LII

**Magical Egypt where are your kings?
You have killed your Gods
and stained your swords**

**You do not honor your sun.
Egypt where the world was forged
In rain and grain.
Where are your Priests?
You have given your history to thieves**

**This our skin of Royal blood
Kings of the Ancient**

LIII

A note for mom.

Her life was a Rose.
Filled with passion and love for the people
She cared for "Those who don't love your family
Can't love you" She would say her dreams are
Made manifest in the lives we lead.
A golden girl that smiles in peace everlasting.

LIV

Fall in love with a Poet, be immortalized
Every inch of you idolized
Your pristine lips, Your curvy hips
Your arresting brown skin
Your wits, your pretty feet
Be besotted with this Poet, you'll see its true.
All living words would eternalize you.

LV

You're finer than Gold
Beautiful, black and bold
My heart is yours, no more closed doors.

I dreamt of something new
For me and you
A future for two like lovers do.

LVI

I walked into the kitchen and watched her,
Her silk Golden hair up in a band
Her feet covered in a woolly pink sock
and her knees holding fast together.

The Sun glowed through her; the leaves bloomed for her
and I am found in the clouds of her air.

I could watch her for hours
Dazed by her unwitting powers,
In her heather Grey sweater.

LVII

Food is more important than time
Even so the little men didn't know
Yet we wonder why Peter pan couldn't grow
The lost boys flew across the snow
like a gust of wind blowing flour and Dough

As shadows they drifted from Post to Post
The Alley cats hissed, and they snarled.
With fangs as sharp as Sabre,
and their hair electrified.
They whooshed across the Night
Never did they divide.

LVIII

All the answers to philosophy
are answered in the silence
of the Questions thought.
Once words are used in description
These answers Question thought

"Don't close your enquiry on the account
Of good so easily. Be a critical thinker?

"Nature is immoral in its Essence
and this is the final truth".

LIX

What is Christianity but a road to heaven

A path to escape this empty Abyss

This consistent overflowing Eternity.

Blessed is he that chooses his own path,

The hermit that creates his own heaven

He that breathes in God new life

and speaks to this Earth his silent truth.

LX

**Do not conform to this zeitgeist,
Beautiful citizens of the sun,
Hell is tiresome normalcy,
Persevere for the liberation
of the spirit.
Do not oppose your ordinariness.
and welcome indifference with
curiosity that endures.**

LXI

**It's all an illusion take a fucking chance
a garbage illusion of security, we are all going to die
Go back to the land with your family,
live as you are.
Do not hesitate, live in your bliss.
Accept your fear and walk within it.
Fear is the warmth of the fire**

On the other side is the death of tragedy
On the other side everything is Zen.

LXII

Philosophy must be the nemesis to nature
An enemy to a blissful state
An exceptionally addictive activity,
That keeps you away from the present.

LXIII

One of the fundamental duties of the mind,
is to justify our wishes, to command Intuition into reality
Primarily, farming is man's best vocation
Only crops can sustain a civilization.
The very process of growing grains
Implants in the society an ethos of
Harmony and gentle pride that nurtures
Kindness amongst its citizens and
Stabilizes the Nuclear family

LXIV

This mountain that fires
This immutable force

What is mind but a Union of
Shadows
A bridge to the stars.

The problem with Philosophy is that it strives to come to conclusions on reason, yet it searches for answers beyond hubris.

The nature of reality is forever
Incomprehensible to the human mind
Yet we indulge the thought.

"What a beautiful way to die
Such a death that calm the earth
A picture-perfect death".

www.ingramcontent.com/pod-product-compliance
Lightning Source LLC
LaVergne TN
LVHW041259150826
845673LV00008B/2658

* 9 7 9 8 3 7 1 4 2 4 0 0 6 *